Usborne English Readers

Starter Level

The Mouse's Wedding

Retold by Mairi Mackinnon

Illustrated by Gemma Román

English language consultant: Peter Viney

Contents

You can listen to the story online here:
usborne.com/mousesweddingaudio

This is the mouse family. Father Mouse and Mother Mouse have one child, little Molly Mouse.

We want the best for our daughter.

Little Molly
has good food,

Yum!

nice clothes,
and lovely toys.

One day, Molly says, "Father, when
can I be married?"

"Let's find a husband for you," says
Father Mouse. "Let's find the best
husband in the world."

"Who can that be?" asks Molly.
"The sun!" says Father Mouse.

The sun is big and strong.

Everyone loves the sun.

"How can we meet him?" asks Mother Mouse. "The sun is up there, and we are down here."

"Let's go up the mountain," says Father Mouse. "In the evening, the sun is near the mountain top."

The family put food and clothes in their bags. They walk to the top of the mountain, and there is the sun. "Hello, Sun!" says Father Mouse.

It's nice to meet you.

"Hello," says the sun. "Who are you?" "We are the mouse family!" says Father Mouse. "My lovely daughter Molly is looking for a husband. You are so strong and bright…"

"Strong?" says the sun. "I'm not strong. Do you see that cloud? He can hide my face, and then it's cold and dark everywhere."

I can't do anything about it.

"Oh!" says Father Mouse. "Well… can we talk to the cloud?"

"I'm tired now," says the cloud. "Please come back in the morning." The next day, the mouse family go up the mountain again. The cloud is near the top.

"Hello, Cloud!" says Father Mouse. "It's nice to meet you! We are looking for a strong husband for my daughter…"

"Strong?" says the cloud. "I'm not strong. The wind can push me here, there and everywhere. I can't do anything about it."

"Oh," says Father Mouse. "Well, let's talk to the wind."

Later, the wind comes and pushes the cloud off the mountain.

"Hello, Wind," says Father Mouse. "We're looking for a strong husband for my daughter…"

"Strong?" says the wind. "I'm not strong. Up here, I can go everywhere, but down in the valley, I sometimes meet a wall. Then I just stop."

I can't do anything about it.

"Well," says Father Mouse, "let's talk to a wall."

"Talk to a wall?" says Molly – but she goes down to the valley with Father and Mother Mouse.

They soon find a wall.

"Hello," says Father Mouse. "We are looking for a strong husband for my daughter…"

"Oh, I'm not strong," says the wall. "Can you see that hole down there? A mouse is making that hole, and I can't stop him."

"Father, can we meet the mouse?" says Molly.

Yes, let's meet the mouse.

The mouse comes out of his hole. He has bright eyes and a nice smile.

"Hello," he says. "What can I do for you?"

"Hello," says Father Mouse. "We're looking for a nice strong husband for my daughter."

"Do you mean me? Am I strong?" the mouse asks.

"Oh yes!" says Molly.

"Everyone thinks the sun is strong, but a cloud can hide the sun."

"The wind can push the cloud, and a wall can stop the wind..."

"...but you can make a hole under the wall, and nothing can stop you."

"That's true" says the mouse. "I can."
His name is Marcus. Molly really
likes him, and he likes Molly too.

Soon it's time for the wedding. It's a lovely day. The sun is bright, there is no cloud and the wind is quiet. Molly and Marcus are married, and Father and Mother Mouse are happy.

We just want the best for our daughter.

All kinds of weddings

In many countries, the bride (woman getting married) wears white.

In India, brides often wear red.

People can get married in churches, temples, mosques...

...or town halls...

...in the open air...

...or under water!

What are weddings like where you live?

Activities

The answers are on page 24.

Can you see it in the picture?
Which three things *can't* you see?

bag bird cloud fish flower mountain
mice sea sky sun tree wind

Is that right?

Which of these sentences are true?

1.

Father and Mother Mouse
really love Molly.

2.

The cloud can stop
the wind.

3.

The wall is on top of
the mountain.

4.

Marcus Mouse has bright
eyes and a nice smile.

What are they saying?

There are some wrong words here.
Can you choose the right word?

1.

chooses   loves   wants

2.

easy   important   nice

3.

about   for   like

4.

cloud   mouse   wind

What can they do?

Choose the right words for the people or things in the pictures.

The cloud

Marcus

The wall

The wind

A.

I can make a hole in the wall.

B.

I can push the cloud here, there and everywhere.

C.

I can hide the sun's face.

D.

I can stop the wind.

Talk about the pictures

Which three sentences go with picture 1,
and which go with picture 2?

A. The sun is bright and there is no cloud.

B. Molly and Marcus are married.

C. Molly Mouse lives with her mother and father.

D. It's a lovely day.

E. Molly Mouse has good food.

F. Molly Mouse has nice clothes and lovely toys.

Word list

bright (adj) when something shines or gives light, it is bright.

cloud (n) clouds are in the sky. Rain comes from clouds.

hide (v) when you hide something, you stop people from seeing it.

hole (n) an empty space, or the space you make when you take something away.

later (adv) after some time.

mouse, mice (n) a very small animal with a long tail.

push (v) when you push something, you make it move forward or away from you.

cloud

wind

strong (adj) when you are strong, you can do difficult things. Sometimes 'strong' means you can move or carry heavy things. Sometimes it means other people can't hurt you.

toys (n pl) children play with toys.

valley (n) the space between hills or mountains.

wall (n) a wall can be a part of a house, or around a garden or a field. It is usually made of stone or bricks.

wedding (n) when two people get married, they have a wedding.

wind (n) air moving quickly in the sky or over the land and sea.

mouse

wedding

Answers

Can you see it in the picture?
Three things you can't see:
fish, ~~tree~~, wind

Is that right?
Sentences 1 and 4
are true.

What are they saying?
1. ~~knows~~ loves
2. ~~strange~~ nice
3. ~~with~~ about
4. ~~sun~~ mouse

What can they do?
The cloud – C
Marcus – A
The wall – D
The wind – B

Talk about the pictures
Sentences C, E and F go with picture 1.
Sentences A, B and D go with picture 2.

You can find information about other Usborne English Readers here: usborne.com/englishreaders

Designed by Melissa Gandhi
Series designer: Laura Nelson Norris
Edited by Jane Chisholm

First published in 2022 by Usborne Publishing Ltd.,
Usborne House, 83-85 Saffron Hill, London EC1N 8RT, England.
www.usborne.com Copyright © 2022 Usborne Publishing Ltd.